BODY ARTS
THE HISTORY OF TATTOOING AND BODY MODIFICATION™

THE CULTURE AND SCIENCE OF IMPLANTS

Monique Vescia

Rosen
YA™

New York

Published in 2019 by The Rosen Publishing Group, Inc.
29 East 21st Street, New York, NY 10010

Copyright © 2019 by The Rosen Publishing Group, Inc.

First Edition

Cataloging-in-Publication Data

Names: Vescia, Monique, author.
Title: The culture and science of implants / Monique Vescia.
Description: New York : Rosen Publishing, 2019 | Series: Body arts : the history of tattooing and body modification | Includes bibliographical references and index. | Audience: Grades 9–12.
Identifiers: ISBN 9781508180647 (library bound) | ISBN 9781508180654 (pbk.)
Subjects: LCSH: Body marking—Juvenile literature. | Body art—Juvenile literature.
Classification: LCC GN419.15 V44 2019 | DDC 391.6′5—dc23

Manufactured in the United States of America

CONTENTS

INTRODUCTION

A widespread cultural practice with a long and fascinating history, body modification has become a highly visible feature of modern life. In the United States, Canada, and other industrialized nations, the growing popularity of tattoos and piercings has inspired many young adults to seek out even more unusual ways to alter their bodies. Developments in technology have made new tools, materials, and techniques available to people who engage in body modification.

Implant surgery is when an incision is made in the skin and a synthetic material is inserted beneath it to contour or reshape certain areas of body. It can be used to change a jawline or enlarge the breasts when a client wishes to augment his or her appearance in conventional ways. Implants can also create highly unconventional effects, such as the appearance of horns on a human forehead or raised designs on the chest and forearms.

Implants are a relatively recent method of body modification flourishing in two very different cultural environments. One of these is a world obsessed with youth and beauty where highly paid plastic surgeons sculpt bodies and faces into idealized shapes. While the majority of individuals undergoing implant surgery have

This implant contains biosensors that can monitor a person's metabolism. It's implanted in a human subject and transmits real-time data via Bluetooth.

been women, a growing number of men now choose to modify their bodies with cosmetic procedures. Since different body types and facial features continually go in and out of fashion, the perfect face and body will always be a work in progress.

The other culture embracing surgery is one in active rebellion against conventional notions of beauty. Tattoo and piercing artists have defied laws and cultural taboos to innovate radically new techniques for transforming the body with subdermal, transdermal, and microdermal implants. Under the skin, silicon body jewelry can sculpt the body into surprising and unnatural shapes, sometimes blurring the lines between human and animal and person and machine.

The celebrities and so-called "influencers" often featured in advertising campaigns link these two very different worlds. They take ideas from the cultural fringes and repackage them for mainstream consumption. They show that the desire to modify one's body occurs along a spectrum and suggest that these two cultural realms are actually not so far apart.

The next frontier in the world of implants will likely be those for medical and scientific purposes. There are prototypes or even working models of implants that can test one's blood chemistry, with the results transmitted wirelessly to a doctor. There's another type of implant that allows the colorblind to "feel" colors. Other working implants include the Eyeborg, a video camera placed directly in the eye, which may be used for filmmaking or other practical reasons in the future. Then there are NFC and RFID implants, which allow for transmission of personal information such as passwords or credit card numbers with the wave of the hand.

For both art and science, individuals have endured excruciating pain and sometimes even performed surgery on themselves to modify their bodies in increasingly more extreme ways. Some practitioners treat the body as a medium for expression that actively seeks to shock and disturb. However, what looks like self-injury to some may actually be a way of celebrating the body and restoring its connection to the spirit. Here, body modification retains pathways to ancient rituals of pain and blood that put practitioners in touch with sacred realms. The very essence of our humanity may lie in our compulsion to keep challenging the idea of what it means to be human.

Finally, there are celebrities and influencers that span those two very different worlds. They take ideas from the cultural edges and introduce them into the mainstream. They show that the urge to modify the body occurs along a spectrum and suggest that these two cultural realms are actually not so different. The very essence of our humanity may lie in our need to keep challenging and changing the idea of what it actually means to be human.

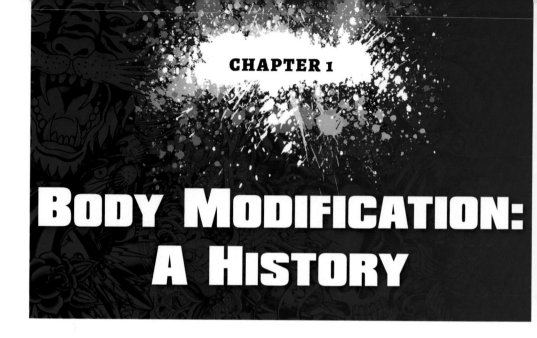

CHAPTER 1

BODY MODIFICATION: A HISTORY

T he desire to alter and adorn one's body has always been a feature of human culture. Viking men filed horizontal grooves into their teeth. In preparation for marriage, Nigerian girls endured the pain of elaborate patterns of scars carved across their abdomens. The Maya, Inca, and certain North American native tribes bound infants' heads to create an elongated skull, possibly a sign of higher social status.

In areas as geographically distant as Africa, South America, and British Columbia, people adorned their lips with large plates, disks, or plugs called labrets. The lip was cut and stretched to accommodate larger and larger labrets, and often the lower teeth were removed to create room for this ornamentation. Despite the fact that these and other modifications may restrict movement or inhibit normal bodily functions such as eating and swallowing, people have nonetheless embraced such practices for thousands of years.

WHY DO IT?

Some body modifications represented traditional acts of cultural identity, while other alterations may have been purely ornamental. The archaeological record shows that body modification has a long history, but in many cases anthropologists can only make educated guesses about the meaning of a specific modification. Descriptions of customs in one culture recorded by individuals from another may be distorted by cultural biases and assumptions. For instance, eighteenth-century Europeans who described elaborate Polynesian tattoos could not understand the larger social context or meaning of this ritual. What looked to them like a bizarre and disfigur-

This woman from the Mursi tribe in Ethiopia displays a range of body modifications, including face paint and stretched earlobes. Her lower lip has been altered to accommodate a lip plug.

ing practice was actually one custom among many that Polynesians believed were necessary for the creation of a complete human being.

We do know that people engage in these practices for many reasons. Some elective modifications represent important coming-of-age rituals, serving to initiate a boy or girl into adulthood. Tattoos or pigment applied to the skin may serve to identify one's social position or signal one's affiliation with a specific group. Certain modifications, such as tattoos and the amputation of fingers, are acts of mourning—a means of commemorating a lost loved one.

Altering the body often has a spiritual significance. Both Jewish and Islamic religious law dictates that circumcision, the cutting away of the foreskin of the penis, be performed on male infants at birth. A newborn baby may seem perfect to many, but some world cultures traditionally believe that humans enter the world as imperfect beings. Therefore, altering the body is essential to the process of becoming fully human.

Nonelective body modification occurs when a person's body is changed or marked without his or her consent. Slave owners sometimes tattooed or branded slaves to mark them as their property and to punish them for attempting to escape. The rule of law might dictate that the right hand of a thief be amputated or someone who slanders another have his or her tongue cut out.

IMPLANTS THAT TEST YOUR BLOOD

Implants are not only for self-expression. They can also be medical lifesavers. Swiss researchers have developed a prototype of an implant that uses sensors to test patients' blood for medical purposes. The sensors can monitor chemicals such as lactate, glucose, and ATP.

The device transmits the results via Bluetooth to the battery patch, located on the outside of the body. The information can then be sent digitally to a doctor anywhere in the world, eliminating the need for doctor visits or having blood drawn. This could be especially helpful for immobile patients, such as the elderly or those with chronic illnesses. Researchers hope to have a commercially available device within just a few years.

The faces of criminals were tattooed to stigmatize them and to identify them to other members of society.

MODERN MODS

Today, humans continue to modify their bodies for a variety of reasons, some relatively superficial and others deeply spiritual. The history of body modification constitutes a visual language that expresses a wide range of human drives and desires, both individual and cultural.

One reason why people choose to modify their bodies is to enhance their physical beauty. Cutting, styling, and coloring one's hair, shaving body hair, painting

Herbert Chavez, who calls himself "Superman's biggest fan," has had twenty-six different plastic surgeries to make him appear similar to the "Man of Steel."

one's nails, and applying makeup are all methods of body modification intended to beautify the body. Unlike these, tattooing and piercing are permanent methods of body modification, not easily corrected or reversed, yet in many communities it has become rare to see a young adult without a tattoo or a pierced navel or eyebrow. A tattoo or piercing helps draw attention to a specific part of the body, such as a toned belly or a muscular bicep, that an individual wants to emphasize.

Implants are a recent addition to the language of body modification. The process is relatively straightforward: an incision is made in the skin and an implant made of synthetic material is inserted inside, changing the size and shape of a specific area of the body. A woman unhappy with the size of her breasts can have them enlarged; a man may have a chin implant to create a stronger profile. This new technology enables plastic surgeons to transform people's appearances to make them seem more attractive. Even a small change may improve an individual's self-image and give him or her more confidence.

CHANGING VIEWS

Human beings have always altered their bodies to conform to cultural ideals of beauty. A stroll through any art gallery will show that concepts of physical beauty have changed radically over time. Nineteenth-century women wore corsets to uncomfortably constrict the size of their waists when a "wasp waist" was considered the height of female beauty. Curvaceous breasts and buttocks may be considered desirable today, but flappers in the 1920s bound their chests tightly to create a more boyish physique, a body type symbolic of the new freedoms they embraced during that era.

What many see as the ideal masculine form has also evolved over the years. Classical Greek statues show a hyper-muscular male form that is back in style today. But during the Gilded Age (late 1800s to early 1900s), weight meant status, so the ideal male body was roly-poly. A beer belly symbolized prosperity.

EXPRESSIONS OF REBELLION

While some undergo body modification procedures in order to conform to cultural ideals of beauty, others choose to change and decorate their bodies in pursuit of nonconformity. Artists and other creative individuals often define themselves in opposition to the society at large. Teenagers have always looked for ways to rebel against social taboos and push the boundaries of what is socially acceptable.

As expressions of individuality and rebellion, tattoos and piercings have long been popular with young adults. A neck tattoo or a tongue piercing once had the power to shock or intimidate. Visible body art could prevent a person from being hired at many jobs. In fact, tattooing was illegal in New York City until 1997.

However, piercings and tattoos have become increasingly common. Public figures such as athletes, musicians, and entertainers with visible body art have accustomed people to the sight of multiple tattoos and piercings. Advertisements featuring models displaying body art have also served to introduce different modifications to the cultural mainstream. As of 2015, 83 percent of Americans had their earlobes pierced. By 2016, 40 percent of US adults between the ages of twenty-six and forty had at least one tattoo.

Even extensive tattoos that cover large portions of the body have lost their power to shock. In many industries, having a pierced nose or sleeve tattoos no longer reduces your chance of getting hired. For some jobs, these body modifications might even make you a *more* desirable candidate. As a result, people have begun to explore forms of body art such as scarification and implants that still retain the power to startle and intimidate.

Scarification is an ancient method of creating body art that has attracted growing interest in body modification communities. An artist uses a scalpel to cut designs and patterns into the skin, deliberately creating scars. Tattoo and piercing artists have begun to add scarification to the list of procedures they will perform.

EVERYTHING OLD IS NEW

Body art implants represent a new technique in body modification, though the origins of this method may trace back to Myanmar (formerly Burma), where people once inserted protective amulets under their skin. Since 1994, when an American tattoo artist named Steve Haworth began to develop new techniques for creating decorative implants, this procedure has been gaining adherents.

Body art implants create 3D designs on the body. Implants require surgery, since an incision is made in the skin, allowing a piece of "body jewelry" to be inserted inside and creating a raised design. The incision is then allowed to heal. Body jewelry now comes

Tattoo artists Victor and Gabriela Peralta appeared in the 2014 *Guinness Book of World Records* as the married couple with the most body modifications. They both have forehead implants.

in an infinite variety of patterns and designs, allowing people to transform their bodies in highly unique and startling ways.

THE POWER OF RITUAL

In addition to the desire to beautify one's body, and for purposes of social rebellion and self-expression, individuals choose to modify their bodies for many of the same reasons that ancient peoples did. For some, it represents a rite of passage into adulthood or a visible sign of one's identification with a particular community.

The practice of body modification belongs to an ancient tradition, and for some, this link with the past feels deeply meaningful. In 1967, an influential body modification practitioner named Fakir Musafar first used the term "modern primitives." In a modern world in which mass culture has wiped out indigenous tribal traditions, modern primitives seek to reconnect with humanity's earliest origins. Painful rituals like tattooing and scarification establish continuity with the distant past and its sacred traditions. The pain that comes with these practices becomes an important part of the spiritual experience.

The decision to deliberately cut, mark, and scar one's body in permanent ways may be profoundly disturbing to some. Others may dismiss cosmetic implant surgeries as acts of vanity that transform the natural human body into a false and plasticized form. But in today's industrialized societies, body modification is a choice, an arrangement freely entered into between a plastic surgeon or a body modification artist and an adult client. More than anything else we may acquire in life, our bodies belong to us. What we choose to do with them and why is a personal decision.

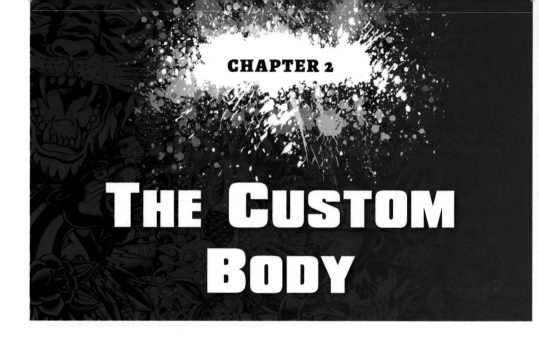

CHAPTER 2

THE CUSTOM BODY

What does beauty look like? The answer to that question is constantly changing. Throughout history, women and men have altered their own bodies to conform to prevailing ideals of beauty. People in many world cultures have willingly submitted to painful procedures such as tattooing and scarification in order to beautify their bodies.

In male-dominated cultures, many women have felt pressure (or been forced) to alter their bodies in dangerous ways in accordance with what men find attractive. In nineteenth-century China, the bound and crippled foot was considered a symbol of feminine beauty.

During the Victorian age, women nibbled on arsenic "complexion wafers" to whiten their skin, despite the fact that they were ingesting a poison that causes hair loss and nerve and kidney damage. Female genital mutilation, performed to ensure female "purity," is still practiced in Chad,

Egypt, Ethiopia, and many other African countries. In the Kayan ethnic group in Myanmar, long necks have traditionally been seen as the height of female beauty. Young girls are fitted with a series of graduated brass rings to form a collar to elongate their necks and compress their shoulders over time, earning them the nickname "the giraffe women." Though the rings are heavy and the practice makes it difficult to swallow, the custom persists.

Though highly poisonous, arsenic was once touted as a beauty treatment to make the skin look pale. Cosmetics manufacturers added it to soaps, lotions, and other beauty aids.

RESHAPING THE BREAST

As early as the 1880s, people began trying to change the size and shape of the female breast. Materials inserted in the breast included ivory, glass balls, rubber, sponges, and even ox cartilage.

During the 1950s, US doctors experimented with different techniques for changing the size and firmness

THE EYEBORG

When filmmaker Rob Spence wanted to create a new type of movie experience, he invented the Eyeborg, an implant that turns the human eye into a video recorder. With ocularist Phil Bowel and engineers Kosta Grammatis and Martin Ling, Spence designed the camera with an electronic eye shell housing, a circuit board, and a transmitter that transfers the data wirelessly, all on Spence's kitchen table! Through the Eyeborg, viewers can experience a true human point-of-view film, complete with glancing around and blinking. The next step is making the device appear human instead of like something out of a futuristic sci-fi movie.

of the female breast. Women allowed doctors and even unlicensed practitioners to inject silicone directly into their breasts. The silicone hardened, sometimes destroying the breast tissue. As a result, some women had to have their breasts amputated. The silicone injections caused pain, skin discoloration, infection, respiratory and liver problems, and sometimes even led to coma and death.

In 1962, Timmie Jean Lindsey became the first American woman to undergo breast implant surgery. Lindsey had consulted two plastic surgeons to have rose tattoos removed from her breasts, and they convinced

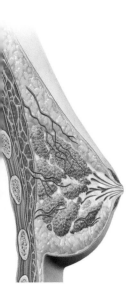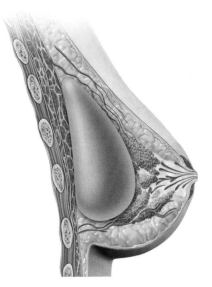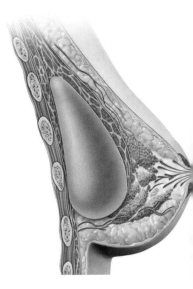

her to volunteer for breast augmentation. The surgeons inserted silicone prostheses beneath the skin of Lindsey's chest, increasing her breast size.

About ten years after the surgery, her breasts began to harden and she experienced shooting pains that plagued her for the rest of her life.

RISKY BUSINESS

Lindsey wasn't the only person to experience dangerous and painful complications from silicone breast implants.

SILICA, SILICON, AND SILICONE

Silica, which is plentiful in sand, is one of the most common materials on earth. Silicon is a semimetallic element found in silica. It has many commercial uses, appearing in products such as plastic and computer chips, which gave Silicon Valley its name. Silicone is a polymer composed of long chains of alternating oxygen and silicon molecules. To make silicone, silicon is extracted from silica and passed through hydrocarbons to create this useful polymer. Like plastic, silicone can be shaped or formed or hardened or softened for many different purposes. Many experts consider silicone safe for cookware, utensils, baby bottle nipples, and toys, but there has been limited research on its long-term health effects.

Following implant surgery, tens of thousands of women experienced hardening of the breast tissue, ruptured implants, and autoimmune disorders.

The first successful lawsuit was filed against Dow Corning, the US manufacturer of silicone implants, in 1977. In 1992, the FDA (Food and Drug Administration) called for a freeze, or moratorium, on the implantation of silicone implants until more research into the safety of these devices could be conducted. By 1995, Dow Corning had been hit with 20,000 lawsuits, and the company filed for bankruptcy.

Two early types of breast implants were made of silicone gel (*left*) and polyurethane (*right*). The technology continues to improve, but silicone is still the implant material of choice.

Due to the moratorium, implants filled with saline (salt water) solution almost completely replaced implants filled with silicone gel during the 1990s. Saline leakage from a ruptured implant poses no known health risks, but the early versions of these implants were heavy and tended to deflate; they also made an audible sloshing sound. Later versions of these implants had lower deflation rates and stronger shells.

As a result of increased government regulation, the manufacturers of implants developed safer devices, subject to government oversight. Manufacturers created a medical-grade silicone gel with a denser consistency, making it less likely to leak. This cohesive gel is a thick and sticky fluid with the consistency of human fat. Implants vary in size, shell thickness, and shape, depending on the final result a patient wants. Most breast implants in place today are "single-lumen," meaning they have a single cavity filled with silicone gel. The shell is made of silicone rubber and typically has a textured surface. Breast tissue grows into this surface.

As of 2017, breast augmentation surgery is still the most common type of cosmetic surgery, and many women are satisfied with the results. However, the procedure is not risk free. Complications can include additional surgeries, infection, pain, scarring, nerve damage, rupture, or deflation. The silicone that leaks after a rupture is not believed to present any health risks, but it may cause pain and changes in the shape of the breast. Following a rupture the implant will need to be removed and replaced. Implants may also shift or be rejected by the body.

A rare type of cancer called anaplastic large cell lymphoma is associated with breast implants. Some women with silicone implants have reported that they suffer from various autoimmune diseases, including fibromyalgia, rheumatoid arthritis, and lupus. While some medical studies have concluded that implants do not cause autoimmune disease, anyone contemplating having implant surgery should fully research these and other risks associated with breast implants.

BODY SCULPTING

A percentage of people undergo implant surgery for reconstructive purposes in the aftermath of an accident or following surgery to remove cancerous masses in

This mannequin at a cosmetic surgery hospital displays nose, cheek, and chin implants. Though used for reconstructive surgery, facial implants are also popular for purely cosmetic reasons.

the body. A woman's breast may be rebuilt following a mastectomy. Someone whose jaw has been shattered in a vehicle accident can regain the ability to eat and speak normally, thanks to facial implant surgery. However, the vast majority of these surgeries are undertaken for purely cosmetic reasons. Such procedures are expensive and come with serious risks, and the patient experiences a painful recovery period. Yet hundreds of thousands of people willingly endure them to radically alter their bodies. Our perpetual desire to change the way we look supports a thriving multibillion-dollar plastic surgery industry.

Men sometimes undergo pectoral implant surgery to give their chests more definition. Plastic surgery can also change the contours of the face with chin, cheek, and jaw implants. As ideals of beauty continue to evolve, buttock (called gluteal) implants have become increasingly popular. The silicone used to create gluteal implants is semi-solid. The procedure involves most of the same risks as breast implants. Buttock implants can also put pressure on the sciatic nerve, causing shooting pains along the back and spine.

Various cultures define beauty in different ways, and implant statistics differ from one country to another. Calf implants, which augment the shape of the lower leg, are common in Mexico and Central and South America, but less so in the United States and Canada.

The procedure for different types of implant surgery is basically the same. During surgery—which may be performed under general, local, or so-called "twilight" anesthesia—the plastic surgeon uses a scalpel to make one or more small incisions in the patient's skin. In the case of breast reconstruction or augmentation surgery, an incision can be made in several places: beneath the breast, in the armpit, in the nipple, and even in the belly button. For gluteal implants, the plastic surgeon may make an incision at the base of the spine between the buttocks, above each buttock, or below at the crease between the buttock and thigh. Incisions are placed to minimize visible scarring on the patient.

The surgeon then creates a path through the tissue of the body to the location where the implant will be placed. The implant is tucked into a small pocket created in the body tissue and positioned carefully. Depending on the desired result, a breast implant may be placed either under or over the muscles in the breast. The surgeon positions the implant carefully to achieve the most natural look. She or he then closes the incision with sutures, which will later be removed or be absorbed by the body. Often small tubes are placed under the skin to help drain off excess blood and bodily fluids from the area during recovery.

Breast and gluteal implant surgery take from one to three hours and do not usually require an overnight stay in the hospital. The patient must wear a supportive gar-

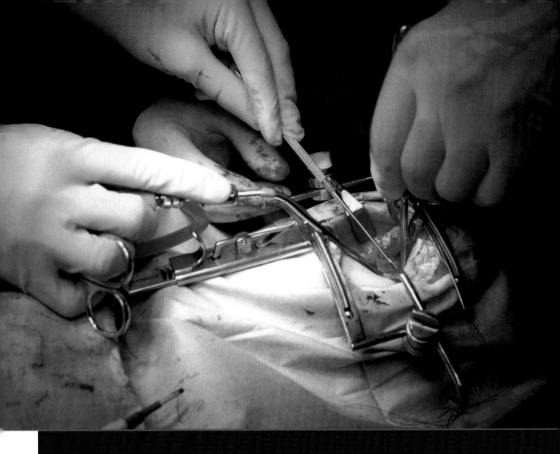

A team of surgeons operates on a patient's mouth. Facial reconstructive surgery can correct birth defects that inhibit a person's ability to speak.

ment for two to three weeks after the procedure. Those recovering from gluteal implant surgery must limit the amount of time they stay seated. Following the procedure, a patient will experience some pain and swelling in the affected area. Most swelling will have subsided three months after the operation.

During facial implant surgery, sculpted pieces of solid silicone, porous polyethylene, or a material known as Gore-Tex are implanted in the cheeks, chin, jaw, or lips.

Polyethylene and Gore-Tex have pores that allow a patient's own tissue to grow into the implants. Facial implant surgery is usually done on an outpatient basis (meaning no overnight stay is required) and typically takes from one to two hours. It carries many of the same risks and complications as other types of implant surgery.

THE DRAWBACKS OF BREAST IMPLANTS

Breast implants may not look or feel like actual breasts, and they can become overly firm in cold weather. Implant surgery leaves permanent scars on the body, which may be visible, depending on where they are placed. In some cases, the body creates scar tissue around incision lines and implants, which is the body's natural reaction to protect itself from a foreign substance. This scar tissue can create a hard and painful lump in the breast, called capsular contracture. Implants can also cause numbness in the breast and nipple.

Breast implants make it more difficult for women to breastfeed their babies, since the implants can interfere with the production of milk. Implants may also complicate breast cancer screenings, and the pressure of a mammogram may cause an implant to rupture.

Implants are not permanent devices; the longer they are in place, the greater the chance they will have to be removed. As breast implants age, the chance of rupture also increases. If implants are removed, the breast tissue may be permanently altered, leaving the skin dimpled or wrinkled.

THE HIGH PRICE OF BEAUTY

Cosmetic surgery is a lucrative industry. Plastic surgeons are among the most highly paid of all medical specialists. The cost for breast implant surgery can range from $5,000 to $9,500. The average cost of gluteal implants is $8,575, but the procedure can cost as much as $14,000. If a patient experiences complications with an implant procedure or needs additional surgeries, medical costs will be much higher.

While medical insurance will often pay for implant surgery for reconstructive purposes, insurers are less likely to reimburse patients when implant surgery is done for cosmetic reasons. Breast and gluteal implants may have to be replaced every ten years or so. Insurance rarely pays for revision surgeries.

Trends in beauty are constantly changing, so the particular body shape or facial feature that an individual has paid dearly for will likely fall out of fashion in the future. The inevitable process of aging and the pull of gravity also take their toll, requiring additional surgeries to restore the youthful appearance a client desires.

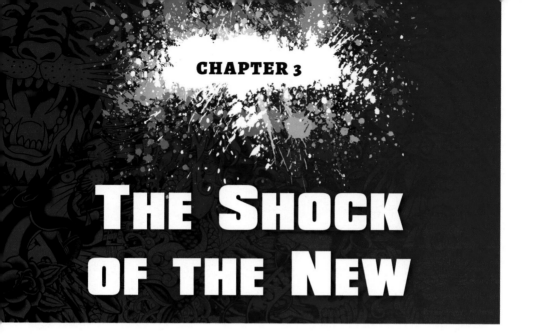

CHAPTER 3

THE SHOCK OF THE NEW

Many people who undergo cosmetic body modification procedures such as breast and buttock augmentation, as well as other types of plastic surgery, typically want their bodies to conform to prevailing ideas of what is beautiful. In contrast, individuals who modify their bodies to display body art may have little interest in being conventionally attractive. Instead, they actively embody new and radical notions of beauty that others may find shocking or even repellant. This may mean getting full-body tattoos that transform their skin into a dizzying canvas of colorful inked designs, or stretching out their earlobes with successively larger ornamental plugs, or gauges.

As people search for more unusual ways of changing their bodies, body art implants have gained in popularity. Since 1994, implant pioneer Steve Haworth has been innovating techniques and teaching implant skills to fellow tattoo and piercing artists.

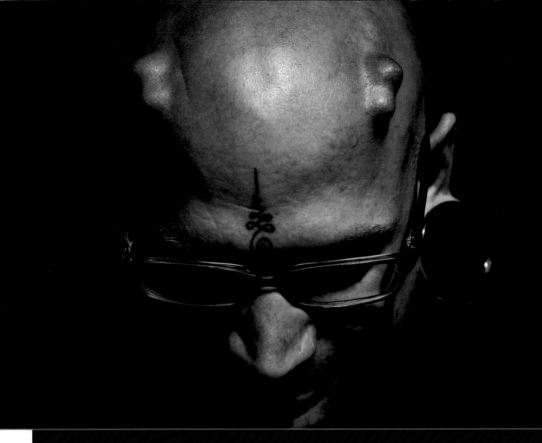

Implants under the skin, known as subdermal implants, create the appearance of horns on this man's skull. An incision scar clearly visible on the left shows where one implant was inserted.

Developments in extreme implant surgery allow people to display horns that sprout from their foreheads, forearms that resemble living sculptures, and shoulders giving birth to stars, skulls, and other shapes. Individuals who sport extreme implants define beauty in strange new ways, transforming their bodies into living works of 3D art.

GETTING UNDER YOUR SKIN

Like cosmetic implants, the first type of extreme implant surgery was subdermal, meaning "under the skin." The

THE MODFATHER: IMPLANT PIONEER STEVE HAWORTH

In 1994, a client challenged the Phoenix-based tattoo artist Steve Haworth to come up with an idea for a "bracelet" tattoo that no one had seen before. Haworth inserted a series of beads under the skin of the client's wrist to create a decorative ridge, performing the first body-art implant. Haworth's 3D body art evolved to include transdermal implant designs like the Metal Mohawk, where a row of metal spikes protrudes from the skull.

Haworth implants body jewelry, made of biocompatible materials such as silicone and Teflon, under the skin to create raised designs shaped like stars, gears, hearts, and even ice cream cones. Haworth is revered in the body modification community as a pioneer and innovator, and has earned a place in the *Guinness Book of World Records*.

body art practitioner makes an incision in the client's skin and implants a piece of silicone body jewelry underneath it, changing the contours of the body's surface. For safety reasons, practitioners have policies about where they will not place implants, such as near the spine, in the back of the neck or on the abdomen, or near moving joints.

While cosmetic implant surgery occurs in a surgical facility, with a certified plastic surgeon operating on an anesthetized patient, body jewelry is implanted by tattoo and piercing artists in their shops or at home. Because body modification practitioners are not licensed to use anesthesia, the surgery happens without it. Someone getting implant surgery will feel pain during and after the procedure, even when ice is used to numb the area. For some, enduring the pain is an important part of the experience.

During the procedure, the artist makes an incision in the top layer of skin, cutting down into the subcutaneous layers of fat. Incisions should be made along the "grain" of the skin. A tool resembling a tiny spatula called a dermal elevator, originally designed by body-mod artist Steve Haworth, is then used to separate the layers of fat, creating a cavity or "pocket" under the skin. The body modification artist then inserts and positions the implant within this pocket and closes the incision with stiches.

As with breast implants, the incision need not be right next to where the implant will be positioned. For example, the incision for an eyebrow implant can be made high on the forehead, hidden beneath the hairline. A pressure bandage or surgical tape over the wound must be kept in place for a week or two while the incision heals. Eventually, the skin heals around the implant.

Horns can be created in the forehead using subdermal implants. The length of the horns that the client wants determines how long the process takes. First small silicone implants are inserted, then gradually replaced with increasingly larger ones, allowing the skin to stretch to accommodate the desired horn length.

TRANSDERMAL TYPES

Transdermal means "through the skin." The transdermal implant is an even more recent innovation in body modification, also credited to Steve Haworth. This type of implant resembles a piercing with an exit, so that a piece of body jewelry such as a metal stud or spike appears to grow out of the body. In 1996, Haworth implanted a "metal mohawk" along the skull of a man named Joe Aylward. Another body

Jeweled microdermal implants sparkle on the shoulders of reality TV star Elettra Miura Lamborghini at the MTV Video Music Awards.

modification artist named Samppa Von Cyborg has since made additional strides in the art of transdermal implants.

During the procedure to create a transdermal implant, the body modification artist makes an incision about an inch or two from where the implant will be located. Dermal elevators are used to create a cavity under the skin where the jewelry will be placed.

Jewelry for a transdermal implant often comes in two parts: the base (or anchor) and the piece (or topper) that screws on to the base. A transdermal implant base typically looks like a flattened pretzel, a figure eight, a cloverleaf, or just a strip with a short bar projecting out of it.

Using a scalpel or a dermal punch, the artist makes a hole in the skin for the bar on the implant base to pass through. He or she then slides the base through the incision and into place. Once the base has been positioned through the skin, the second part of the implant is screwed into place and the original incision is closed. For a design with multiple pieces, such as a metal mohawk, this process must be repeated many times.

MICRODERMAL IMPLANTS

The most common type of implants are microdermals, which are less invasive than subdermal and transdermal implants and involve fewer risks. Microdermals resemble transdermal implants, in which an anchor is implanted below the skin. The metal anchor is oblong in shape and implanted using a dermal punch, which creates a pocket under the skin. A decorative metal topper attaches to the anchor and rests on the skin's surface. The anchor has holes in it, and as the modification heals the skin will grow around these holes. Microdermal implants heal like standard piercings and can be placed anywhere on the body. The toppers are interchangeable, so many different jewelry designs can be attached to the anchors.

"Skin divers" are an alternative to microdermal implants. These look like tiny barbells, with a thin center and larger rounded ends. Because skin divers come in one solid piece, they do not have interchangeable toppers that can be switched out when the wearer wants to change her or his look. Skin divers aren't as firmly anchored as microdermals and have a tendency to pop out of the skin.

SILICONE JEWELRY

Body jewelry made of implant-grade silicone, inserted beneath the skin to create different raised effects on the surface, now comes in a wide variety of designs. Anarchy symbols, musical notes, seashells, and hand grenades are just a few of the designs clients choose to have implanted under their skin.

Implants may also be crafted from a variety of biocompatible materials, including surgical steel and titanium. Sometimes such implants are positioned to enhance the effect of a tattoo on the skin's surface. New trends in implants include the insertion of LED lights under the skin. Small magnets implanted under the skin of the fingers allow someone to "magically" pick

A miniature implantable light emitting diode (LED) is small enough to pass through a needle's eye. Such devices have been implanted into the brains of mice for neuroscience research.

up paper clips and other pieces of metal.

One type of body jewelry currently banned in the United States are eye implants. Dutch eye surgeons have pioneered the implantation of tiny pieces of specially designed jewelry into the mucous membrane of the eye. Since the membrane is clear, the implanted jewelry can be seen through it against the white of the eye.

IS IT LEGAL?

People who practice dermal and transdermal implanting often begin as tattoo and piercing artists. They learn techniques from another artist and practice their skills by "freelancing"—working on clients willing to be experimented on. Because they perform surgery but are prohibited by law from administering anesthesia, implant artists operate in a legal "gray area." This body art technique is relatively new, so laws haven't yet been passed to regulate it.

In fact, no single federal law regulates tattoo and piercing artists in the United States. Nearly every state has some type of body art law, but the regulations vary widely. In 2013, Arkansas passed a bill to limit "nontraditional" body art procedures such as implants. As of 2017, body art implants (with the exception of microdermals) were banned in the state of Oregon.

However, most states do agree on age limits. At least forty-five states prohibit minors from getting tattoos, and thirty-eight prohibit minors from getting tattoos or piercings without a parent's permission. In 2008, the city of Winnipeg outlawed implants because of public health concerns about the spread of infection, making it one of the only places in Canada to ban body modifications beyond piercings and tattoos. Practitioners often worry that creating laws to tightly regulate extreme body modifications will only drive practitioners underground and put their clients at risk.

Many US states require that body modification artists obtain a special license in order to practice their business, which usually means obtaining a certain amount of training in their field. Artists may be required to take classes in blood-borne pathogens, human anatomy, first aid, and CPR. They must abide by the laws of the state or the county where they operate. An unskilled practitioner who makes

IMPLANTING YOUR INFO

Imagine no longer having to carry around your wallet or your keys. That's the idea behind radio-frequency identification (RFID) and near-field communication (NFC) implants. Inserted in the back of the hand or in the wrist, these devices can be waved in front of sensors to unlock doors, transmit credit card information, store passwords, or relay any other data that can be sent electronically within a short range. Imagine unlocking a door just by being near it or paying for a bag of potato chips by just walking past the cash register.

even a slight error can do serious damage to a client's lymphatic or nervous system. Anyone interested in an extreme modification should find a body modification artist who is highly experienced in implant surgery and who works with sterile tools in a sanitary environment.

Some practitioners travel around the country to modify clients in different regions. During an initial consultation, artist and client should discuss the final result the client hopes to achieve as well as the cost of the procedure, which can run from $500 to $2,000 for a single implant.

The body art practitioner should fully explain the process, as well as possible risks and complications and what removal of the implant would involve. Such a consultation also gives the practitioner the chance to determine if the client is mentally imbalanced or otherwise impaired. In some states, body modification artists must turn away a client who is under the influence of drugs or alcohol.

THERE ARE RISKS

As has been shown with breast implants, the process of inserting a piece of synthetic material under the skin can be done safely. As far as we know, no one has ever died from obtaining a body art implant. However, any type of implant surgery carries a risk of serious complications. Proper aftercare, such as keeping the sutured area clean and dry, is important with all types of implants.

BLOOD-BORNE ILLNESSES

The most dangerous risk is the potential of being infected with a blood-borne disease such as HIV or hepatitis B or C, via contaminated blood present on unsterilized instruments. If a scalpel or dermal punch has been previously used on a person infected with a disease and then not properly sterilized, pathogens can be transferred to the next client. HIV is a mutating retrovirus that attacks the human immune system, leading to autoimmunodeficiency syndrome, or AIDS. The symptoms can be treated but no known cure yet exists for the disease. Hepatitis B can lead to liver cancer, liver failure, and death. Hepatitis C is a viral infection in the liver that may result in fatal liver disease. As with AIDS, both types of hepatitis can be treated but not cured.

REACTIONS, REJECTIONS, AND INFECTIONS

Clients should try to stay in good health, which diminishes the chance that the body will reject an implant. If this happens, the implant will push through the skin and have to be removed. After implant surgery, infection is always a possibility, as well as nerve and muscle pressure and shifting of the implant. A client may suffer an allergic reaction to the material being implanted, which can range from mild to severe.

Tissue resorption is another problem that may arise. Subdermal implants are not fused to anything, which means they will constantly rub against the tissue surrounding them or that they rest on. Eventually, that tissue will erode.

Healing can be especially problematic for transdermal implants and may take up to two years to complete. Because the implant site is open to the environment, some of these implants never fully heal, leaving the original wounds surrounded by scarred and irritated skin. Complications include inward-traveling infections, which can eat a hole in the skull.

The success rate for transdermal implants is only about 20 percent. There is a high risk for rejection even after the implant has healed. Because jewelry extends

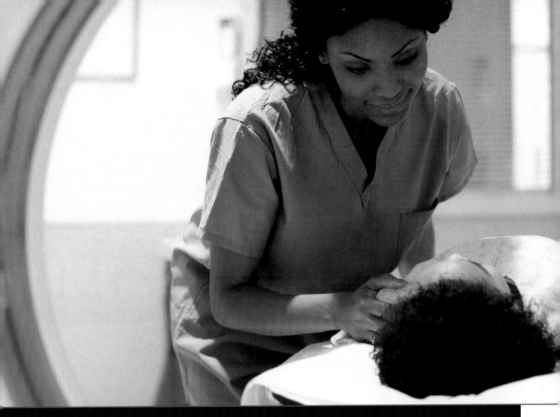

A nurse preps a patient prior to an MRI. The patient's body must be free of all metal in order for the diagnostic technique of magnetic resonance imaging to be used.

out from the body, it can be bumped, which may stimulate reinjury or rejection. Due to scar tissue, removal of transdermal implants is even more difficult than implantation.

ADDITIONAL COMPLICATIONS

One serious drawback with transdermals and microdermals will occur if a client needs diagnostic medical testing such as an MRI or a CAT scan. Since imbedded pieces of metal interfere with the medical equipment, these implants must be removed. For this reason, microdermals and skin divers have been banned in some US states.

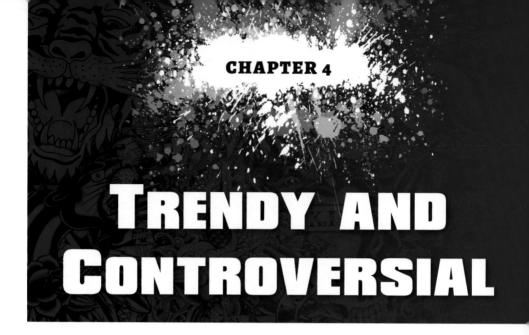

CHAPTER 4

TRENDY AND CONTROVERSIAL

In the United States and other industrialized cultures, people are often obsessed with celebrities. They consume information about the private lives of actors, models, and musicians and closely scrutinize photographs of them. They "follow" them on Twitter and Instagram, and the vast reach of these and other social media platforms means that tweets and images can be instantly viewed by millions of eyeballs. Fans who want to emulate a famous person will eagerly adopt fashions and fads that they see that person sharing on social media.

In Katherine Dunn's disturbing 1989 novel *Geek Love*, followers of Arturo the Aqua Boy willingly submit to amputations to become more like their hero, a circus sideshow attraction who was born with flippers instead of arms and legs. Since the novel was published, the phenomenon of body modification has moved into the cultural mainstream. Celebrities are trendsetters and

Hip-hop artist Lil Wayne displays facial tattoos and dental "bling" onstage at a music festival. He is one of the most-followed rappers on Instagram.

"influencers" who have played an important role in the normalization of body modifications such as tattoos and piercings. They appropriate types of body art once practiced at the fringes of culture and give it wide exposure.

The actress Jessica Alba and the pop star Britney Spears helped popularize modest modifications such as navel piercings; the musical artist Rihanna has twenty-five known tattoos, including *Never a failure, always a lesson* inked across her chest. Former basketball superstar Dennis Rodman is known for his mul-

"FEELING" COLORS

Imagine being able to feel colors. That's what colorblind artist Neil Harbisson set out to do when he invented the Human Antenna, a device that translates colors to vibrations with a camera mounted on his head. Though it started out as an external device, Harbisson eventually had it implanted into his occipital bone, at the back of his skull. The vibrations associated with different colors resound through the bone, and the sensation spreads throughout his skull.

tiple piercings and tattoos. Hip-hop artist Lil Wayne and singer-songwriter Adam Lambert as well as musicians in the bands such as Linkin Park and Incubus have showed off ear gauges that stretch increasingly larger holes in their earlobes.

REGRETS, I'VE HAD A FEW

In an image-obsessed culture such as Hollywood, people often resort to plastic surgery to enhance their looks or to erase the signs of aging. *American Idol* runner-up and political candidate Clay Aiken has had jaw and chin implants to change the shape of his face. Actor Rob Lowe has had chin implants, and the rapper Iggy Azalea and TV star Kylie Jenner have had buttock implants. Many deny rumors that they have had such "work" done, insisting that their attributes come from a healthy lifestyle and good genes. (Revealing "before" and "after" pictures often tell a different story.) In 2011, the reality star Kim Kardashian had her buttocks X-rayed to disprove rumors that her famous curves were the result of implants.

However, some celebrities and actors do admit to having plastic surgery and to having procedures reversed when things go wrong. Pamela Anderson and Victoria Beckham have both gone public about their decision to have their breast implants removed. Some women

The physical appearances of celebrities such as *American Idol* contestant Clay Aiken are under constant scrutiny.

chose to have their implants removed after suffering discomfort and pain, and others complained about getting sick all the time while the implants were in place. Frank discussions about the complications from implant surgery can help inform the public about the risks of these procedures.

WHEN IT'S AN ADDICTION

A condition called body dysmorphic disorder, or BDD, can lead to plastic surgery addiction. A person with this psychiatric condition will fixate on an imagined physical flaw, typically in a facial feature. Their obsession with this "defect" will disrupt their normal activities. They may spend thousands of dollars on a succession of plastic surgeries, trying to achieve an imaginary and impossible ideal. Responsible plastic surgeons screen their patients to determine if they suffer from such a disorder.

Clearly, unscrupulous practitioners can be found who are willing to perform multiple surgeries on a patient addicted to these procedures. Fans of the late Michael Jackson saw the musical superstar's features gradually transform over the course of his career: his skin color lightened from a warm brown to a parchment white, the shape of his lips changed radically, and a cleft appeared in his chin. Jackson seemed obsessed with changing the shape of his nose in particular. He had so many surgeries that ultimately he was left with almost no nose at all.

Dennis Avner, aka Stalking Cat, underwent multiple plastic surgeries and received brow and lip implants to transform himself into his "spirit animal," a female tiger. His extensive body modifications made him notorious and earned him a place in the *Guinness Book of World Records.* Avner's friends say he was a deeply troubled man, and psychologists have speculated that Avner, who apparently took his own life in 2012, may have suffered from BDD.

PLASTIC CELEBRITIES

In today's world of reality television, some individuals have capitalized on their obsessions and become plastic surgery celebrities. Pixee Fox and Justin Jedlica, who style themselves as a real-life

Dennis Avner (aka Stalking Cat or Cat Man) welcomes visitors to an exhibition at Ripley's Believe It or Not. Facial implants contributed to Avner's radical transformation.

Barbie and Ken, met and bonded over their shared obsession with plastic surgery. Jedlica has had more than 340 plastic surgery procedures, including shoulder, back, bicep, cheek, and gluteal implants. Fox has had

Justin Jedlica and Pixee Fox pose proudly with their award for Most Inventive Plastic Surgery at the Aesthetics Show in Las Vegas, Nevada.

numerous breast augmentation surgeries and hip and gluteal implants. She has also had six ribs removed to give herself a sixteen-inch Barbie doll–sized waist.

BODY MODIFICATION OR MUTILATION?

Body modification has been present in every culture since ancient times. Cutting, piercing, and otherwise damaging the body are often associated with healing, spirituality, and maintaining social order. Tattoos and multiple piercings have become so commonplace that among young adults

HARDCORE: ELF EARS AND FORKED TONGUES

The desire to be different drives some people to seek out ever more extreme types of body modification. Two modifications embraced by hardcore practitioners include ear pointing and tongue splitting. Ears can be made pointy by cutting and reshaping the ear or by inserting subdermal implants at the top edges. Tongue splitting or "forking" involves cutting the tongue in two from the tip to as far back as the base. The end result gives the client a forked tongue like a snake or lizard. Not all practitioners will agree to perform this modification for a client, and some people have split their own tongues. People who have their tongues split may have difficulty speaking after the procedure. As of 2017, tongue splitting is banned or strictly regulated in Illinois, New York, Delaware, and Texas, as well as in the US military.

an unmodified body has become the exception rather than the rule. Nonetheless, many people in developed countries find body modification appalling. They are deeply disturbed by such practices, and they wonder why anyone would subject themselves to such painful and disfiguring procedures. Is the desire to radically change one's body actually a form of self-mutilation? What is the difference between people who allow someone to slice into their skin without anesthesia and people who repeatedly cut their own wrist?

Visual artist Maria Jose Cristerna, known as the Vampire Woman, boasts an astonishing array of body art, including horn implants made of titanium.

In general, body modifications are voluntary, and mutilations are involuntary. People who modify their bodies do so for adornment, self-expression, and other positive reasons. They show off their tattoos or their sculpted bodies, whereas individuals who engage in cutting and other forms of self-mutilation are typically ashamed of these actions and try to hide the evidence of it. Someone who feels compelled to mutilate his or her own body does so because of stress or an inability to cope.

Extreme body art will always invite controversy, in part because body modifiers defy taboos in their search for unique modes of self-expression. If history teaches us anything, it is that some human beings will never feel.

GLOSSARY

AUGMENTATION Enlargement.

BIOCOMPATIBLE MATERIAL A natural or synthetic material designed to function along with living tissue.

BLOOD-BORNE DISEASE A disease that can be spread through contamination by blood or other bodily fluids.

BODY ART Art made on, with, or consisting of the human body. It was one of the earliest forms of artistic expression.

BODY DYSMORPHIC DISORDER (BDD) A mental condition in which a person obsesses about one or more perceived flaws in his or her appearance. This obsession with appearance and body image impacts the person's ability to function in daily life.

BODY JEWELRY Jewelry used by body modification artists, including ear, belly, and nose rings, ear gauges, labret and lip studs, microdermals, and silicone implant designs.

BODY MODIFICATION Deliberate altering of the human anatomy or physical appearance, which may include tattooing, piercing, implants, or scarification, as well as cosmetics and hairstyling.

GENERAL ANESTHESIA Drugs or gases used during a surgical procedure to relieve pain and alter consciousness.

IMPLANT Something implanted in body tissue.

LOCAL ANESTHESIA A drug injected at the site of an incision to relieve pain during an operation.

MASTECTOMY Surgical removal of all or part of the breast.

MICRODERMAL IMPLANT A form of body modification that gives the appearance of a transdermal implant without many of the complications. Sometimes called a "single-point piercing."

MORATORIUM A waiting period set by an authority.

PATHOGEN A bacterium, virus, or other microorganism that can cause disease.

PLASTIC SURGERY Surgery to repair, restore, or improve a lost, injured, or defective part of the body.

PROSTHESIS An artificial device to replace or augment a missing part of the body.

SALINE A solution of salt in water.

SILICONE A chemical compound or polymer made up of a chain of alternating silicon and oxygen atoms.

SUBDERMAL IMPLANT An extreme body modification placed under the skin to create a raised design.

TRANSDERMAL IMPLANT An extreme body modification in two parts: an anchor implanted under the skin and a topper that threads onto the anchor. Gives the effect of jewelry screwed directly into the body.

FOR MORE INFORMATION

American Society of Plastic Surgeons (ASPS)
The Plastic Surgery Foundation
444 E. Algonquin Road
Arlington Heights, IL 60005
(847) 228-9900
Website: http://plasticsurgery.org
Founded in 1931, ASPS is the largest plastic surgery specialty organization in the world. Its mission is to advance high quality care to plastic surgery patients by encouraging high standards of ethics, training, physician practice, and research in plastic surgery.

Canadian Society of Plastic Surgeons
PO Box/CP 60192 Saint-Denis
Montreal, QC H2J 4E1
Canada
(514) 843-5415
Website: http://plasticsurgery.ca
This nonprofit professional society represents plastic surgeons in Canada. The society is devoted to improving the quality of patient care through education, outreach, and advocacy.

Centers for Disease Control and Prevention (CDC)
1600 Clifton Road
Atlanta, GA 30333
(404) 639-3311

Website: http://www.cdc.gov
The leading federal agency dedicated to protecting the nation's health, the CDC provides information on the health risks of various body art practices for both clients and artists and how to minimize them.

Penn Museum, "A World Tour of Body Modification"
University of Pennsylvania Museum of Archaeology and Anthropology
3260 South Street
Philadelphia, PA 19104
(215) 898-4000
Website: https://www.penn.museum
Founded in 1887, the museum is the largest university museum in the United States and one of the world's great archaeology and anthropology research museums. The museum's website provides a guided tour through objects in its collection related to body art.

FOR FURTHER READING

Bliss, John. *Preening, Painting, and Piercing: Body Art* (Culture in Action). Chicago, IL: Raintree, 2011.

Cohen, Robert. *Body Piercing and Tattooing.* New York, NY: Rosen Publishing, 2013.

Currie-McGhee, Leanne K. *Tattoos and Body Piercing.* Farmingham Hills, MI: Lucent Books, 2006.

Currie-McGhee, Leanne. *Tattoos, Body Piercings, and Teens.* San Diego, CA: Referencepoint Press, 2013.

Lukash, Frederick N., MD. *The Safe and Sane Guide to Teenage Plastic Surgery.* Dallas, TX: BenBella Books, 2010.

Mercury, Maureen, with photographs by Steve Haworth. *Pagan Fleshworks: The Alchemy of Body Modification.* Rochester, VT: Park Street Press, 2000.

Mifflin, Margot. *Bodies of Subversion: A Secret History of Women and Tattoos.* 3rd ed. Brooklyn, NY: Power-House Books, 2013.

Rainier, Chris. *Ancient Marks: The Sacred Origins of Tattoos and Body Markings.* New York, NY: Earth Aware Editions, 2006.

Thomas, Nicholas. *Body Art* (World of Art). London, UK: Thames & Hudson, 2014.

Vale, V., ed. *Modern Primitives.* 20th anniversary ed. San Francisco, CA: RE/Search Publications, 2010.

Wilcox, Christine. *Teens and Body Image.* San Diego, CA: Referencepoint Press, 2015.

BIBLIOGRAPHY

Adams, Dallon. "8 Bold Biohacks That Blur the Line Between Human and Machine." Digital Trends. May 20, 2017. https://www.digitaltrends.com/cool-tech /coolest-biohacking-implants.

Associated Press. "Cyborgs at Work: Swedish Employees Getting Implanted with Microchips." *Telegraph*. April 04, 2017. http://www.telegraph.co.uk /technology/2017/04/04/cyborgs-work-swedish -employees-getting-implanted-microchips.

The Conversation. "Is Extreme Body Modification Even Legal?" March 3, 2017. https://theconversation.com /is-extreme-body-modification-even-legal-73242.

Currie-McGhee, Leanne K. *Tattoos and Body Piercing.* Farmingham Hills, MI: Lucent Books, 2006.

Eyeborg Project. "About the Project." Retrieved November 14, 2017. http://eyeborgblog.com.

Favazza, Armando, MD. *Bodies Under Siege: Self-mutilation, Nonsuicidal Self-injury, and Body Modification in Culture and Psychiatry*. 3rd ed. Baltimore, MD: Johns Hopkins University Press, 2011.

FDA.gov. "The Risks of Breast Implants." Retrieved October 4, 2017. https://www.fda.gov/MedicalDevices /ProductsandMedicalProcedures/Implantsand Prosthetics/BreastImplants/ucm064106.htm.

Frontline. "Chronology of Silicone Breast Implants." PBS.org. Retrieved October 12, 2017. http://www .pbs.org/wgbh/pages/frontline/implants/cron.html.

Guynup, Sharon. "Scarification: Ancient Body Art Leaving New Marks." *National Geographic*, July 28, 2004. http://news.nationalgeographic .com/news/2004/07/0728_040728 _tvtabooscars.html.

La Carmina. "The Future of Extreme Body Mods: A Chat with Steve Haworth," Huffingtonpost .com, March 11, 2013. https://www.huffingtonpost .com/la-carmina/future-of-extreme-mods_b _2412592.html.

Laura. "The Psychology of Body Modification." March 20, 2015. https://info.painfulpleasures.com/blogs /psychology-body-modification.

Layton, Julia. "How Transdermal Implants Work." How Stuff Works, April 3, 2015. https://people.howstuffworks. com/culture-traditions/body-art/transdermal -implant1.htm.

Medicalbag.com. "Subdermal Implants Come in All Shapes and Sizes," April 14, 2014. http://www .medicalbag.com/body-modification/subdermal -implants-come-in-all-shapes-and-sizes /article/472437.

Mercer, Marsha. "How Safe and Sanitary Is Body Art?" *Washington Post*, June 25, 2017. https://www .washingtonpost.com.

Preidt, Robert. "The Hottest Trend in Plastic Sur- gery." Health Day, CBSNews.com. February 29,

2016. https://www.cbsnews.com/news/the-hot
-new-trend-in-plastic-surgery.
St. Leone, Lori. "The Art and History of Body Modifica-
tion," *Lightspeed Magazine*, November 2010. http://
www.lightspeedmagazine.com/nonfiction
/the-art-and-history-of-body-modification.
Thomas, Nicholas. *Body Art* (World of Art). London,
UK: Thames & Hudson, 2014.
WebMD. "Cheek, Jaw, and Chin Implants" Retrieved
October 3, 2017. https://www.webmd.com/beauty
/cosmetic-procedures-cheek-jaw-chin-implants#2.
Whalen, Sydney. "Subdermal Implants: Understand-
ing the Risks of This Controversial Body Modification
Trend," June 19, 2017. https://www.zwivel.com/blog
/subdermal-implants-body-modification.

INDEX

A

Africa, 8, 19
AIDS, 41, 42
Aiken, Clay, 46
Alba, Jessica, 45
amputation, 10, 20, 44
amulets, 15
anchor, 36, 37
Anderson, Pamela, 47
anesthesia, 27, 34, 38, 51
anthropology, 9
archaeology, 9
Arkansas, 49
augmentation, 4, 21, 24,
    26, 27, 31, 49
Avner, Dennis, 48–49
Aylward, Joe, 35
Azalea, Iggy, 46

B

Beckham, Victoria, 47
biocompatible material, 37
blood-borne disease, 39,
    41–42
body art, 14, 15, 31, 33,
    39–41, 45, 52
body dysmorphic disorder
    (BDD), 48, 49

body jewelry, 6, 15, 33,
    35, 37, 38
branding, 10
breasts, 4, 13, 19–21, 22,
    24–27, 29, 30, 31, 34,
    41, 47, 49
British Columbia,
    Canada, 8

C

calf implants, 26
celebrities, 6, 7, 44, 47, 49
Central America, 26
cosmetic procedures, 6
criminals, 11
cultural identity, 9

D

Dow Corning, 22
drainage, 27
Dunn, Katherine, 44

E

Eyeborg, 7

F

facial implant, 26, 28, 29
Food and Drug Adminis-
    tration (FDA), 22
Fox, Pixee, 49

ABOUT THE AUTHOR

Monique Vescia is the author of numerous nonfiction books for young people on a wide range of subjects, including *Mahatma Gandhi: Champion of the Indian Independence Movement, Scientists at Work: Engineers, Choose Your Own Career Adventure on Broadway*, and *The Rise and Fall of the Byzantine Empire*. She makes her home in Seattle, Washington.

PHOTO CREDITS

Cover, p. 1 Jim Varney/Science Source; p. 5 Amelie-Benoist/BSIP/Corbis Documentary/Getty Images; p. 9 Robert Pickett/Corbis Documentary/Getty Images; p. 12 Jay Directo/AFP/Getty Images; p. 16 Yasuyoshi Chiba/AFP/Getty Images; p. 19 © The Advertising Archives/Bridgeman Images; p. 21 Leonello Calvett/Stocktrek Images/Getty Images; p. 23 Yvonne Hemsey/Hulton Archive/Getty Images; p. 25 The Washington Post/Getty Images; p. 28 Jean-Marc Giboux/Hulton Archive/Getty Images; p. 32 Marka/Alamy Stock Photo; p. 35 Steve Granitz/WireImage/Getty Images; p. 38 Professor John Rogers/University of Illinois/Science Source; p. 43 ERproductions Ltd/Blend Images/Getty Images; p. 45 Rick Kern/WireImage/Getty Images; p. 47 John Lamparski/WireImage/Getty Images; p. 49 Jemal Countess/WireImage/Getty Images; p. 50 Barcroft Media/Getty Images; p. 52 Hector Guerrero/AFP/Getty Images; cover and interior pages Liubomyr Feshchyn/Hemera/Thinkstock (splatters), Gollfx/Shutterstock.com (tattoo design).

Design: Brian Garvey; Layout: Ellina Litmanovich; Photo Researcher: Nicole Baker